CACTUS

By the same author:

Sweetened in Coals (2014)

Diwurruwurru: Poetry from the Gulf of Carpentaria (2015)

Borroloola Class (2017)

Fume (2018)

CACTUS

PHILLIP HALL

RECENT
WORK
PRESS

Cactus
Recent Work Press
Canberra, Australia

Copyright © Phillip Hall, 2021

ISBN: 9780645008968 (paperback)

A catalogue record for this
book is available from the
National Library of Australia

Cover image: 'the collectivity' by Ellie on flickr.com, reproduced under
Creative Commons Attribution Licence 2.0
Cover design: Recent Work Press
Set by Recent Work Press

recentworkpress.com

MD

For
the love with whom I fly:
Jillian (XXX);
mum & dad (Joan & Ray);
Rhiannon/Jason, Aidan/Jessica, Ceinwen, Kian/Brooke;
my first grandchild
(yes, I am so joyfully a Popeye);
Lyn & Peter
Melissa, Rachel, Nicky, Amanda Jane, Derek
(& their families);
& my brindle boy greyhounds who have rescued me:
Charlie Brown & Billy Blue

In loving memory of:
Samuel, Matthew & Danny
(my heart breaks
for all who know the burden
of grief)

Contents

Acknowledgement of Country

Cactus

Acknowledgement of Country

Sky-Country

for the Kulin Nations

...swept to scudding mist and manna,
to the white trunks of a slurred-over terrain,
the huge dark wing beats are a skirmish
of creation pouring out from the grey spiraling steam
as talons are thrust forward in a lunge
at ground zero before vertical recovery skids
to apex and another soaring
U-shaped dive that tears
earth by its roots, raising
country out of a blue-smoky spray
now sweet with the scent of eucalyptus and mint:

blooming in a bowl felted, and warily
watched over by another's shallow-beating and quivering
charcoaled wings, the sinuous curves of country are cherished
in a loud descendant wailing that gushes
open all the streaming waters and creatures of our time...

Cactus

The Sunshine Line

(The breath in our nostrils is a puff of smoke,
put this out and our body turns to ashes,
and the spirit melts away like idle air.
'Come then, let us enjoy what good things there are,
let not one flower of springtime pass us by,
before they wither crown ourselves with roses.'
The Book of Wisdom 2: 2-8)

Anxious and in the way (like all
                 suicide survivors)
    I lay out my woolly vintage
VFL guernsey (the talisman for getting me
out), Bulldog Charlie's red, white
                 and blue oasis
amidst all the canneries, railway yards and rubber factories;
here Scraggers plied their trade
in wonder at the centre bounce
and an epic bronze on the basalt plinth is Mr Football's archetypal
                 torpedoed clearance:

    In this shadow I ricochet, stooped
in fancy, bent over a ball bobbing from my fingers,
              swerving at full speed
as collision lifts and buckles my body,
        loosens teeth from a Chesty Bond jaw:

        And my breathing again pings
with facial tics so, I raise a hand
      to hide an open mouth   inhaling deeply
           before the bear-like exhalation   escapes:

Over coffee I am scored
for Henryk Gorecki's *Third Symphony*,
    ecstatic lamentation cradled
    in folk drone, a melodic missive pressed
    downwards as lower strings are bowed without diminuendo,
and cleaved to this primitive tonality
a soprano's towering expressive charge—
        this is a canon, sounding genocide:

And my anxieties manifest in obsessive cleaning of a toilet, crawling
    after hairs and fluff in corners
before housework gives way
    to R.M. Williams: black merino crewe (beneath
my talismanic guernsey), moleskins, leather belt and boots:

After some more made-up care
    I am (almost) set to go; an amble into Sunshine,
    and the train to Flinders before a walk
up Swanston to Melbourne Museum and *We Call Them Vikings*:

    I set out on Suffolk and Hampshire Roads where
weatherboard cottages are now adorned with dragons, golden
    Vietnamese welcome and Buddhist grottoes
to our Holy Mother; here front gardens are a crop
    of corn, pumpkin, pomegranate and lime
amidst succulents, cycads and roses; and Ballarat Road congregates
late arrivals in mosque and gurdwara, whilst *Sudanese Harmony* settles
    between *Thien Nhi Bun Bo Hue* and *Walia Ibex - Ethiopian Café*:

I've been prescribed medicine and footy cards to disrupt
    grog's glumness
    but it's Sunshine, despite Liberal slurs of gang horror,
that is the earthly paradise—my
        lemon balm and chamomile:

Last weekend Western Bulldogs hosted
the Ujamaa Festival to rise
        with *#AfricanGangs*: drumming, dancing, henna,
food stalls and face painting before an evening of fireworks,
a constellation's blazing packed
        crowd for AFLW—and I was up
                        in tears:

On the train between Sunshine and Flinders I stand
        guarding anxieties between friends
(my club colours) and I smile
        at the welcome of strangers: *Go Doggies*
        giving my rejoinder: *woof, woof, woof*
such small things
        to render a line:

        I'm on a day out
though paid sick leave has given way to
unemployment, so I write for nothing, stumped by the endurance
of family whilst I hunt return
                as household manager:

Last night I watched Time Team's three days
dig on Fetlar Island: a looted boat burial
        with one surviving trefoil brooch transformed
        for a goddess; and a longhouse's collapsed mass
guarding a blue schist floor, soapstone (loom
and fishing net weights); but most precious
                a longhouse's buried escape tunnel—
these boat people were no fearless pirates
but small, fretful farmers home to stay:

And Neil Oliver fashioned people
as a flow apart, where dead bodies hung in branches
and flamboyant hairstyles attracted
        immortal standing, this blizzard of flashing axes
driven into the sea by a glacier's irresistible
        action so that a new start became grounded in trade: arctic
furs, amber and oils; but in England the Danelaw
broke in Anglo-Saxon xenophobia
and Ethelred the Unready's St Brice's Day Massacre
        where a longhouse's souterrain escape
was a mass grave:

        With Wagnerian anticipation
Melbournians queue before a museum's recreated
        Oseberg ship, and there are iron axes, but Aryan
eugenics is a desolation of monsters and giants; whilst glass cabinets
hoard weights and measures, grindstones,
board games; and grave goods are not axes but a
Frankish glass beaker, Irish cross, Indian statuette of Buddha,
Coptic ladle, and
beads of carnelian and rock crystal; while trefoil brooches
        are gilded silver, reimagining
                baldric and sword decoration:

Before these displays, I falter
        towards oblivion, remembering
I am no longer trusted
home alone with grog and knives, but in truth
I'd never foul my own nest as self-harm is self-care, well
a leeching anyway, and my suicide
is always a walk alone into space, a suppressed
escape route with a hoard of empties to mark a valetudinarian's
        ceremonial way, and not a treasure anywhere
        from my Doggies or family to show where
                                I once withered   with a crown.

The Passion of Cards

for Martin Axelsson & Steve Wang

Pulling into Flinders Street Station I'm on guard
against all those four-litre, fourteen-dollar casks
        once secreted into the corners
            of my home,
grog's mouthful giving
              license to mischief:

        Exiting
    the station I need to pee
so, bee-line to the NGV
I only work
          in a clean stall:

  Now I channel spirit
into footy cards, considering
      the cost
 of each indulgence against
         another cask not drunk:

Consequently, I have a calling
     to Card Zone and should
have departed at Flagstaff but don't know the way
         so awkwardly
   I pick a path the length of Swanston:

    My consolation:
not tempted outside Clocks at Flinders
(a welcome bar) where Mirka Mora drenches
        my morning in irreverent, wide-eyed
       children, animals and angels   all captivated
in a longed-for garden mural:

At home I now count
                change openly
my family teasing, which card my new quarry:

                I collect
only Doggies (female and male),
                and arrange each token
in guernsey number so
                with each purchase the whole
collection must be freed
                and reassembled:

This album travels
                close, a passenger
        of cards against pints;
                it gathers signatures, medals and cups
and is a portrait gallery
                of an evolving player list as I track
                        down those who managed a handful
of breakout games before injury's cull; and from these sleeves

                        proof I belong.

Bacchus In Ruins

*(As meals are made for laughter, so wine gives joy to life
but indiscretion sprouts wings. Ecclesiastes 10:19-20)*

The Luftwaffe exposed
Bacchus beneath rubble, twice born of fire and nursed in rain
a liberated, fluid boundary, lounged in disarray
the grace of Bacchus is our release
into pleasure, where prayers
to a fennel staff topped with a pinecone might
adjust unshackled abandon   and
                        sadness:

'In drinking wine, we drink him' wrote
Euripides in The Bacchae, but in this contest
to be the 'one true vine' I have drowned
in fundamentalism rushing to rub myself out, to empty
cask and glass in the mirror
                      of precepts: 'to thine ownself be true':

I am soursob weeded shit
sniffed on unwashed fingers, and I thirst
to gape camel-like at hubris and catastrophe
ah, I resent every day surrendered
to moderation, the guttural groaning
that celebrates order, a life denuded
                   of ecstasy   and defeat:

I am fallen
not to revelry, but to self
hatred, lust
      for transcendence, and my appeal
for guilt free suicide   is the poured libation
             of metastasis   with treatment denied:

Nonetheless, I still love all those
suburban honeyeaters under clear
blue, spring rich skies, but
even in sunshine, my worth is shrouded
    and I'm stuck   self-medicating against
                            the blue.

Hymns of Thanksgiving at the Existentialist Café

(after Soren Kierkegaard & Philip Glass)

I

lit from behind
the shoulder   a porthole
onto black woollen turtleneck   a single profile
of Sisyphus spurred on to evermore
fear and trembling   scales
of uncooperative melancholia—*teardrops
in the furnace*

II

resume composition
and resign to insult   or
surrender to
herd virtue—*nerve is
wildfire*

III

after the shudder of three days silence
Abraham laid his hand
on the boy's head and drew
his knife
this is the burden
of loving a god—*narcissism strikes deep
it starts when you sleep*

IV

to cast aside
living like a cipher
in the crowd   as bad faith
(to be Caesar   or nothing)
to dump cargo
in order to drive the price   to window dress
domestic violence
as Torah proofs for faith   these are cowardly
haggling over what is fair and square—*all the years*
I've given you   thinking you wanted me

V

conversations between left and right
hands   mercurial sonorities
like the stronghold
of chords
the ambient starkness and sweep
of a cutback   anguished drone—*why*
does someone   have to die

VI

collaboration is the revelator in the canon
of Glass
where too much freedom is a mechanism of
oppression   and anxiety is
the main course
a treat of yoga with vegetarian pie—*it's time*
we made time   just for talking

VII

providence is unwelcome asylum
in this café of
milk and honey
and a dying son's wounds   for our fragility
only underscore a father's
heart of stone
who seems to never turn the other cheek
in a cosmos where despair is unforgivable—*self-medicate*
with cold gin   as red scriptures
are no heaven-sent knocking   at your door

The Moment of Death

is   as significant as taking a dump, there are no
prayers, no new age
trite words beyond words

My partner miscarried in a public hospital's toilet
& forever after I have dreamt
of ashes, my ashes, flushed down
that same space

I have unwrapped another baby
born too soon in an afternoon's bloody mess
of wrenched bedding

I had a brother, broken and leaking, die
fallen in scenic wonder and collected in my lap
the unraveling   long wait for air
ambulance retrieval

Another in hospital with tubes
& drugs and stuff   it was my decision
on doctors' advice, to turn off
life support and watch
the colour drain

Perhaps because of our rather baroque
sacramentality, I am addicted
to aesthetic minimalism, to a vigil
suffused with the labored breathing of the dying   breath
that falters   in farewell

Mine is the failed breath of those keeping watch
the strain of nostalgia, the incandescence
of loss

But the closest I now get to any
ascetic tradition of ecstasy and insight
is lifting things
at the gym, or drunkenly
slicing up my thighs to tip my toes
in the pool of blood coagulating
neatly on the floor

(in memory of Samuel, Matthew & Danny)

what to do when
you've been loved to judge
there go I but for the grace of God when
you are no longer 7 or 14 or 21 and
you've woken to smell the roses
where then do you go

Unforgivable

(May it please God to crush me,
to give his hand free play and do away with me!
Job 6: 9)

Well, there are at least a thousand reasons why
I despair (and in the recurring nightmare
many more) where
a troubled night after drinking
alone gives way to grunge
and a surrealist's caved-in cranium, the clear
brain fluid frothing
with snot and leaking
from every orifice
in a head once held dear
to me.

The Good Samaritan

I had four university graduations I desperately wanted
and worked hard to attend   but went to none
the dread of humiliation in public
was a fact felt more
than my own name   inevitable
like life or death   to hide
inside neatly packaged roles   resisting the deathly pull
of a way out   I am beat   stuck
in a mud of anxiety   and there are (oddly)
universes to love   such a trunk of goodness
I do not wish to die   to halt
in failure   but
the railway tracks all end
in hurt   though I lived to be

a donor

professional development

at the end of every school term I bragged
there should be nothing left held dear
every identified need must
be met, no child left
behind   I was
fucked

sulky

with the smallest amount
of grog on board   I squeak

and now my body has corrupted
my breathing
into a chesty
shortness that fails
to adequately expel
carbon dioxide   and hiding behind a raised opened hand
facial tics are all the worse
for being made
self-aware   libido goes belly up   and now
I am a night time teeth grinder
with eighteen pearly whites
needing either extraction or filling

I feel laughable
and now my body buckles and
trails

bruxing: a mouthful of hurt

noon
and already finished my first bottle of cheap red
I indulge the doleful
mouthful   the un-knowing
grinding of myself   to keep it under wraps
this drive to hurt   it takes one
to know one
and I know   brew   I will hang
my head low   teardrops
to pickle the jam of
staying alive

kith 'n' kin

I am cheap red
wasted   why am I
not enough   as though
sobriety is worthiness or
a slack dick   I stay alive
only for others   in a family
where grief is fresh
laid shit   how
can I multiply ache
surrender to the disassembly
line's crush gates   the blubbering
is this   I need an end
but am pitiably/providentially/jacked in
to gold

Gongoozler's Lament

I am a multiverse resident, living indecisively
on the slide, and my new ache
    is for UK narrowboats and slow
            off-grid, canal living:

I cast myself as broken-down, solo
crank where my trad stern and hull
are in need of good pressure washing, but a steel hatch
is security, and solar
might be drilled and bracket-bolted between
a roof's pigeon boxes and brass mushroom vents,
and a one-tonne, vintage diesel engine has a throttle wheel
and leather drive belts that chug along
like a well-oiled and serviced navvy's post-industrial
arcadian dream, and I still
        make my bed
     nightly in a boater's fold-out cabin:

Before the traditional Epping stove
I fortify myself against the sober cold   dreaming
of fresh black hammerite paint, and a new set of anodes, to harden up
against corrosion's pitting of my hull; and I pipedream
spare pistons, bearings and rings
to give me continual
cruising up the cut at two-miles an hour, coupling
the industrial mid-lands with this green
        and pleasant plot:

I need to slow down, to get lost
afloat in postcard beauty, to somehow
rediscover resilience   worthy
   of living:

So, I plug away, indulged
between swans and herons, but ducking
dreaded conviviality; I have my own
rhythms for approaching swing
bridges and locks, for cleaning
a composting toilet and bilge tank, and I obsess
like a fly-by-nighter, over this engineering knack
          for shifting tonnes:

A staircase lock works
by equalising pressure, raising or lowering
        payloads, and I wonder
   will I ever have my own oak-lined cabin, guarding
loneliness   behind stern and bow fenders.

and the crows can have my eyes

I am too indecisive to do
        what needs to be done, but I can
envisage an end
when a winter expedition with an unburdened pack
sets out from Katoomba into scenic wonder
        Glen Raphael's to Narrow Neck Plateau
        where morning mist can come spilling
        over swampy heaths and I can hit
after a few days hiking the junction
of the Cox's & Kanangra Creeks, from there
it's a walk in the park to the Deep
        where some whiskey can ease
a crossing into cold, bleak
bush—a guilt free passing kept carefully from view.

sacred ground

to wield the knife is one thing
but what if all that's done
a spot in harm's way

What I Would Have Missed

...it hurts, this drive
to end   why
isn't this Attenborough wonderland
enough   I have family and my place
at home, muscles and passion
to be useful, but still
there's a brilliance that fails
to graft   I've tried to beat
it, drink it under
or cut it out   I've yielded
to my daily pill, to appointments
with nice people concerned
holistically with me   while others have tested
my estrangement from God and the lure
of 'false prophets'   and my atheist
partner (whilst I dither, hoping for God to show signs
of life, to demonstrate change
to just cause) has bribed me with gold
membership of a footy club that wins
nothing but hearts   but we turned up
and a dam wall burst
with more tears than could possibly fit in two
premiership cups   I've been paid off
with the stars and stripes
of Hawktail String Quartet, such Appalachian zip
untethering the heart-
land from centre stage   but still
to my shame and amidst so much
I am weak for an end...

blood lust

why do I need blood
to leech from my thighs and pool
at my toes, to make plain
the pain I feel

why does my spirit stress
greater secrecy for the gashes
I have made than for my own

anus   I am ashamed, and addicted
to slashes   entrances
onto me

but still I want my children (&
their partners) to process
past my naked scarred, stiff trunk

                    and see me

one-legged dog

(after The Wrestler:
a film by Darren Aronofsky
& a song by Bruce Springsteen)

I

no more the boss   my drive
to self-harm is likely to end
in care   how to shield the act
of cutting from snooping
restraint   to ram
relief through this quarrel
with blood

when you're on the ropes
it's what hits   the floor

II

the film
opens in tableau by-line glory
a hundred kilo of gift-wrapped muscle
though steroids have broken
his heart
& a nose-dive milked
for all it's worth
is an old school low shot
ending in a trailer park where toxic
push and shove
The Passion
pantomime of brutes & idols
all crowned by a staple gun's thorns &
razor wire under the spotlights
of the ring   an ear-splitting mob

adoring the best of him
scapegoat on the
ropes

III

as credits roll
his aging burnt
scarecrow bling
a gravel pit
of piercings & black leather
spoiling bruise

bet you slump   a one trick pony
when the blood hits the floor

Dark Matter

with Gillian Welch & David Rawlings

There's this christ person parable concerning talents
    and whiskey and the underside of prickly
        bushes, radioactive blame
    when others should be thriving because
of your work, when wailing
              is finding yourself pensioned at home:

Everyday I'm getting calmer (a decision nearer), sleeping
      with pills, watching the frets scored
to an instrument's thighs, darling remember
           what might have been, working
    a love song luxury, bled
        like red scripture:

I have been blessed
with so much, ring those bells
like an air-conditioned road train captain roaring
and a top paddock clipped
to bulk billed order, such baggage ground under
      accelerator to herd return:

    What possibilities might
tomorrow bring when the chasing of wild ponies
    is picked, precipitous loss; the droning, double-stops
      and syncopated bowing of Appalachia; a laid down ensemble
pallet pressed to earth floor?

This front porch is
national public radio where gospel is alien
to drum machines and synthesised
mirtazapine, and a miscarried birthright has the bent of dirt
music, guitar and banjo picking circles, fiddled
improvisation where even the sinking broke
                tremor deeply
      like a double bass doghouse   bulging
                           at the seams.

A Valetudinarian's 'Crisis' in a Time of COVID 19

for the progressive bluegrass of Punch Brothers
arranged in the old-fashioned way
(on a magic carpet
around a single mighty mic)

I am indebted in lock-down more than ever to my partner safe at home
but also, more a cock on the lookout
whose ensemble overdrive is measured
in teaspoons of vegemite or crushed garlic
or in mugs of strong black coffee hiding
the bottle of pre-noon comeuppance that makes bearable
the reels and jigs of perfidy and moonshine
soaked up in a sofa's distressed leather:

I am unshaven, daggy
in worn black and grey tracksuit and
holey woollen socks, shying away from the world
dog-tired from that damned earworm jingle
of what   I've become:

I wish to look at home
in check or plaid or flannel, to be practised
with power tools and solvents whilst commiserating
in a convivial evening's 'Hops of Guldenberg'
or amidst other such booze-soaked hymns
but all I now get is an empty inbox
as I turn over and over to 'punch brothers punch
with care'.

Unhinged

(As wounding strokes are good medicine for evil
So, blows bring healing to the deepest self.
Proverbs 20: 30)

I

I would wed an earth goddess
and be king—
my manicured hands 'future proofing'
against drought and storm.
I would wed a cut
throat in the bog—
go willingly to an overkilled crown
have my nipples cut to saga.

II

I am a beaten
prodigal youth worker in need of wreckage
like that
consented to in Gethsemane, the longed-for
torment
of the Stations of the Cross.

III

And in these gardens where sacrifice of self
is unhinged,
sinking like a moth to the Dead Marshes'
flickering light,
prowess is plain
in manacled hands, and braided
leather and bronze armlets are a copper-alloy
Brownlow, where to play on
with three broken vertebrae or punctured
lung, is a substitute
for worth.

IV

What is it to cast male
order/woe
on a pile of self-harm, to weep
from the scarification of your thighs
and chest like the tapping of
latex from trees?
What is it to confess the elation of wounds
still bleeding
after two weeks?

V

And so, I am pricked
along with shadows, straightening
spirit and flesh,
while surrendering to a cyclopean devotion at the forge
where club colours are pounded
in contest and crisis
before the release of a grand final parade
and a male binding
with hazel withies before being cut
and struck down in an exhaustion's rallying
when a siren's tears might just dump
manhood
in the shade
of a premiership cup.

on   crying

                                        wolf

            I   too

                    I   fear

waving   not drowning

                            I   fear

Flash Art

for Rosalie Gascoigne in the NGV

I sit, back against
the cantilevered opening that was once my Beer DeLuxe, to consume self
indulgence in long black and lemon tart
> a sorrow diagnosed as separation from God, though a partner's
> constancy is the cladded marvel
of Fed Square's sandstone, zinc and glass; a carbon neutral, catered
> coherence within triangular
>> pinwheel grids:

> I am outside
> the NGV's hermetic seal
having outlived professional
usefulness, a pensioned
pile of retro-reflective discord
and half-understood assembled
> jigsaw precariously propped
> in the verge:

At Rosalie Gascoigne's *Flash Art*, I stammer
towards entropy and corrugated bitumen blasted
> bushfire light; a cache
of geometric and retro
ravaged lines recycled
> in a beehive's golden crossword
>> and concrete poem:

Later, over more coffee and cake, I shape up
> to this joy in signage, grand
> and redundant
>> on a gallery's walls.

Splintered Assemblage

(Catching the Indian Pacific to Rosalie Gascoigne's 'Monaro')

I am fossicking through my bucket list, transcontinental
adventure kitsch
where all-inclusive opulence
means: I don't lift a finger; and crafted
brass detailing is a bitter-sweet
acacia's bumblebee bloom:

Just before boarding
an anxiety attack has me foundering
maybe a daughter could be spirited away, saving me
but a partner's discreetly attentive firmness
ushers me to a luxuriously appointed suite:

In truth, my odyssey is the Viking trail
from York to Orkney Islands, but scared
of flight I have outlived
usefulness, like this classic age of rail, so I prowl
the trackside ditches of mental decline for poignancy
in rusty corrugated iron,
the bricolage of Rosalie's dried thistle stalks:

On this train the booze is 'free'
accordingly, I'm soon scotching along
with George Mackay Brown's *Collected*, and crying out
against idiot-royals and that orange trumper fool, upsetting
decency and reaffirming beliefs
sorry, I'm bloody useless:

Thank god for Americans who are overpaid and over here
        a young widowed, champion
        sailor with two daughters and an admiral dad,
            and a retired teacher couple who'd actually known
            Ursula Le Guin: they gave me incentive to whisper
sober into winds like a wizard of Earthsea fleeing
            foul shadow-beasts in the delight
                of Laser Class single-sailor dinghies:

        I am my own worst enemy, frustrating
verbal recognition in anxieties and cryptic clues, searching
for secrets in Rosalie's assemblage
        of fragments propped precariously:

Because, even amidst this railway luxury and indulged
            bubble, the shadow
I carry is a cardboard
            coffin and surrender:

And so finally, I enter the gallery
            where a collection is a beehive's royal jelly,
the wheat-field of arcadia
waving across Rosalie's bands and grids to cross-hatched tesserae
and herringbones of narrow strips, here to be airborne
is a cache of recycled, battered and worn
mass produced packing cases, stenciled with brand names,
                and cut with her band saw into ever thinner slivers:

Here, the scratch marks
            are the bold and ungentle joy
        of wanting in.

Call Me Legion

(after Stanley Spencer's paintings:
'Christ in Cookham: Christ calling his disciples'
& 'Christ in the Wilderness')

I am again reading some apocryphal
      gospels on gallery walls, searching
              for Stanley's traces of a kind and wonderful
fool amidst all this twenty-first century's muscular
      christianity:

For Stanley, the Cookham twelve are belligerent players,
their cross-armed biceps
              bullying a child's hopscotch to fenced-in edges:

He anticipated the rise of evangelicals as overheated harvesters
      who order their empty baskets out to a loop
              of wind and willow, while still raising a host
to pleasant escapades, diverting charges of hypocrisy
with cozy woolen jumpers and squashy cushions,
              sowing the seeds of their righteous
                    nostalgia:

Whatever happened to stray innocence-of-heart, to bumbling
      along a path with disciples left enlightened?

    Now Christ is really in the wilderness, condemned
to sackcloth, where even the resurrection
           is a comfort banished to the perimeters of their
                    moral majority.

From Hans to Nora, with Love

(after the NGV exhibition:
'Hans & Nora Heysen: Two Generations of Australian Art')

I had a season ticket
to a father's (unfounded?) dread of a lockout from love, when
what was intended as unconditional, is felt as hurt
        strings attached:

      I wanted an exhibition's curated fatherliness,
bespoke nurture, all or nothing
      picture perfect love, but I got
          award-winning lines of demarcation
(landscape for him/portraiture for her):

A migrant success, Hans made The Cedars his prosperous
      family homestead, the endowment
of South Australia's fashionable, where the sun
      was therapeutic, rustic spirituality
and sinuous organic forms were an Arts and Crafts hallowed
      interior design; and solace
was acquired in nurturing trees from tiny suckers
        to sturdy, closely knit bulk of old age:

He instructed that conventional composition should shy
away from experimentation as lacking discipline
thus, he embraced the daring
ways of academic copyist:
        Dutch Masters, Symbolism and Art Nouveau:

And his sense of proportion was praise
for landscape's monumental geometric shapes, the impulse
        to rugged, stifling heat:

In his home, a daughter met monumental
                    gums, fragrant
bourbon roses, lilacs and irises in the cosseted
overwhelming sublime, but father feared growing
aghast at her maturity: venturesome enterprise
        in cosmopolitan self-portrait,
        a crumpled ambiguity
in work trousers and army uniform, such meticulous French loosening
                    and higher-keyed chic:

And her Archibald winning itch
met bursting hubbub from a fraternity
that knew everybody's place, as she pitched
curvaceous promise alongside the sway
                            of emancipated vigor:

Nora had no illusions of glory
but kept to the pure delineated features of her sitter, luminous
with pleasurable and productive   heroic
        hues in a match
        to an overshadowing, yet gentle, genial father.

I Am the Vine!

(Bacchus in the Antipodes)

Prologue: When Jews for Jesus Call on the Oracle of Springwood

(after Norman Lindsay at home in the Blue Mountains)
for Leslie (Pa) Aaron Gordon Hall
grandson of Rabbi Aaron Alexander Levi
> *(a widower who struggled with depression & alcohol dependency*
> *& first cantor in the Great Synagogue of Sydney)*

Pa and dad were chapel small, upholsterers who barracked
for the herd, and news of the death of God
never arrived, furthermore
when at the home of Mr & Mrs Lindsay for work, inducement
to sinful peeping away from the sitting-room's
deep buttoned antiques and model boats
must have been pondered as alien
but Pa—that Jewish whiz raconteur—always returned
to rich, roaring laughter and impeccable
manners, and Mr Lindsay always paid on time:

Over the years, Mr Lindsay gave Pa little gifts, one
was a luxuriantly illustrated and inscribed book, a personal memoir
of Springwood Olympus by a Mr Douglas Stewart (who Pa met
one weekend when delivering some work); Pa detected
my contrary flow, my hard
love with dad, I grew to his gentle words and gifted book—
> anxieties arching over us
>> like a bond:

In this book I met Norman's feckless charm and formidable
saintliness dressed as an irascible devil's scamp; and quarrels
leapt from crag to crag as his Roman beaked nose sniffed out
a cautionary Atlantis (decadence & cataclysm) that might have bled
from our *Revelation*; I was fastened
               like a spiritualist   haunting
                                        Flanders:

But my yo-yo relationship with bohemianism
               was doomed (the Baptists had the child, so owned
the man) and, anyway, Pa was forever
               at our breakfast table with toast and pots of tea, cheering us on
with his Oliver Twist stories of himself as Jewbo—
               such hurt phylacteries pride manifest
as our patriarchal archangel, fiddling on the roof
                              of what we might become.

I: *Springwood Olympus*

(Norman Lindsay: 1879-1969
or Ubermensch in The Land of the Golden Fleece)

Theirs is a gunfire breakfast and Mediterranean
      climate luxuriating in the cavalcade of bush
      spirits and riotous protectionism with a bent
for ad-libbing and hullabaloo
in sandstone Romanesque villa complex
              with narrow bullnose verandahs:

      Such a clutch of golden drowsiness
in terraced gardens, but the pool is leak-prone
      and darting around ionic columns
there's a satyr pursuing nymph in strength
      through joy—boudoir fantasy, criminal climax:

This fiery faith in puffery
      reawakened in caress
      and libidinous release is their overblown
nostalgia fouling common sense:

      And a colossus is wished-for
      to straddle the Heads in bellicose
anti-modernism because muscle
      is eugenics and eurhythmics, the weight
to prey on wowsers, while Hyperboreans fix
      a sun on ripening fruit and unbroken
              masculine happiness:

In their Hellenism, rollicking visions
        of anglo-artist-men as gods; miserly and spindly
        saplings untrammelled by gum tree tyrants,
are a wistfully melancholic   faded
zooming superman   harbour idyll   mesmerized
        by a pure, healthy race
        of mirror men
                never grown flaccid.

II: *Homer's Sorceress*

(Bertram Mackennal: 1863-1931
or Circe Delivers)

Daphne was his perfectly proportioned wet dream
inciting divine violence   excused
    by him as she is arrested
at the moment of transformation/flight
           into a tree, her closed eyelids
           his projected, erotic frisson:

And his *Diana Wounded* is a flesh-and-blood beauty
a coy and lissome, unclothed, modern (Edwardian) woman, spied on
    and bent over in the act of 'removing'
garter or stocking—a poeticized (in Bronze)
           'nude girls' neon:

Such hypnotic, scale and swagger
in bronze abundance of alchemy, like a charm
that he expects will return those full-blooded, voluptuous types ready
           for capture:

And *Circe* seals the deal: a high-stakes, full frontal
nude on an ornamented relief drum; her feet and hips squared,
head garlanded with asps, and commanding
outstretched arms rigid in their pride

        witchcraft

      this is his cautionary tale
      as her demonic, engulfing force
    has chaotic man tumbling from grace
and fornicating, swinishly, amidst all those coiled snakes.

III: *Goulburn Odysseus*

(Sydney Long: 1871-1955
buried somewhere in London's Streatham Cemetery)

Such a charming, great fibber of short
gammy stature, masked under an anglophile's
                                          top hat and
            sinuous line:

I imagine his self-portrait framed by misadventure
            as he is strapped to a mast
            of evangelical enmity, the church siren squabble
of unhinged contrary winds:

He is enthroned, a lavishly robed
            cave-in of doubt, while behind him a halo
is dissolving twilight, the dancing
            crooks and curves of naked, translucent
                        youths silhouetted against the lyrical sweep
            of foggy melancholia:

            His is a Gumnut Nouveau, bitter
in the detour of gothically
illuminated and acclimatized
            nymphs and naiads, a bucolic lilting slope
            transforming reeds and water lilies
                        into the pipes of Pan:

            Amidst these rhythmic serpentine necks
of brolgas and flamingoes, a pond reflects
            a raging bushfire, and from the silhouettes
of spindly trees   a shadowy rivulet
                        bleeds canvas dry.

IV: A Satyr's Thumbs-Down to a Laughless God

(Frank (Guy) Lynch: 1895-1967
And this Doom of Youth)

...cross the Sydney Opera House forecourt and enter
gardens near the Man o' War steps, there's a Gallipoli veteran
with shaggy-haired, cloven-hoofed legs
and well-muscled pagan lust rocking
back on his bronzed haunches, eyes shut deliciously
in post-coital ease, semen pearling
                                                        from flaccid cock...

V: Sunbaker

(Max Dupain: 1911-1992
These Strapping Sons of Neptune)

With a son and daughter ripening
on the vine, and a wife for teething infants, his revolt
      against the herd assumed the weight
of an afternoon's sun struck torpor:

      His was the perfect, muscular glory
an impulse to disrupt the flywheel
of mechanized, murderous war; to return man
         to a lifesaver's drills, patrol and parade
where a march past could again be a flourish of speedos and caps
fastened under chesty bond jaws:

He had seized the antidote to degeneracy and nightmares
      trench stuck in an order both natural
and fortunate for him; her indrawn demeanor and gift of breasts
      animating luminous spill, a glowing band
           arching through his dreams:

   In this lineage
of classical proportions   he was lucky
      like one of the gods and their gang charging
         through surf
      —honorably discharged—
    in the ease of a manly, sunlit afternoon.

VI: The Boy, Ares

(Jack Lindsay: 1900-1990
Writes 100 books & Dreams us Peace)

Of all the Lindsays reveling in their picnic
of acclimatised gods, the one I dreamed
      was Jack, fleeing home
                     to far off
           English shores:

     A precarious childhood
      in a brood abandoned
by the Oracle of Springwood who had found a younger model wife
        Jack watched mother drink
a hurdy-gurdy babble, sheering shame, as he pleaded
       to be plebian and worthy
               to father's aristocracy of talent:

For father, blood was spirit
and ubiquitous, he was leery
and demoralized in a Flanders fathomless brutality,
      the darker torments of a shadowy
satyr's lacerated mind:

Stuck in a scum of horror
father forced a way; he attacked Modernismus
      in a one man Renaissance
           —I affirm Life/I affirm Beauty—
and in the Ouija board he (desperately) re-erected
              the bones of family faith:

And from this taxing, bombastic banner
                    snagged in the barbed-wire deterrence
at the Gap's brink, Jack begged permit
but he had chosen a path
            of deviationist sin (compassion)
so would remain to father a shameful, fringe phenomenon.

Epilogue: Aphrodite's Renaissance

for Judith Wright
& Alma (Nana) Hall née Taylor

Nana was no Flapper
Pa didn't like cheeky girls; he wanted a shy
life as his father was tanked-up
so, before you could say 'Jack Robinson', Pa fell in love
looking her up and down: 'you know' he said
'if I found the right girl, I wouldn't ask her to change,
                                        I'd follow':

Ironically, Aphrodite incited Norman
more than Pa; She was a bugle-call, calling-out
bluster, She opposed wowsers too, but His manifesto
to remake only traumatized, broken
white men into hyper-vigorous, sinewy hero-artists was a false start
                        and no gain at all:

His invocation of classical bodies
was a dazzling cardboard fake and impasse
where hoplites mounted pedestals
of concrete boots while She was forever foil
                                to a gallery of villains:

She was no shy nana, and like Norman, keen
to abandon old-fogeyism and castoff
constrictive clothing, but unlike Him, She would claim
a sure-footed and shared
fitting together, She would rejoice with Nana in the scattering sparks
            of their own   voyage out.

Where the Bee Sucks

(a matador's vitalism)

I am home in Sunshine
              basking
        in John Olsen's memoir
where a Paul Klee line is flowing homage
in space
        to *Under Milkwood*'s village surrealism:

              This memoir is also, however, a loutish
paring away and distortion
        of line to breathe in
              homophobia and sexism   corrupting
        the translucent
juicy-fruit, frazzle-dazzle rat-race
              behind a beret-crowned head:

              As I step
        into Sunshine
              to travel to his *You Beaut Country*
Charlie Pippett's monumental, wrought
        iron gates once opened to the harvester works
where a railway's junction now meditates
              a Four Kindness Stupa:

        And shoppers now flicker
between Vietnamese greengrocers
and Sudanese Harmony and Billiards Café,
where Tet is a welcome
of incense and strings of red firecrackers,
and the front yards of weatherboard bungalows are now adorned
              with dragons, shrines and good luck altars:

In the main street, John Kelly's *Man Lifting Cow* is bronzed
WW II comical camouflage laboring
                in overalls below a bovine milk carton
with Joshua Smith neck and that cheeky
        'win a wish' horned and nodding head
        which today rejoices in offerings
                        of red envelopes and lanterns:

        On the train,
between Sunshine and Flinders, I am exuberant
looking out for Doggies tags (Now it's always 2016!)
        when an Aboriginal flag beats
                        with concentration: NO PRIDE IN GENOCIDE
and I am pricked by Olsen's line: 'Aboriginal
art has gone to the dogs' (what premierships we keep in mind):

        At Fed Square I stretch
out the egg-yolk, freckled-rapture
                        of the sun, taking in
this couple-coloured world, this joy
in juice, on a day when Trump has won
                and certain incivility is a tide of itinerant eyes:

At the NGV I am ticketed and good
to go, though a memoir's
                        values are a byline's jerk:

                Stepping in,
a gallery's monochrome and arid walls are transformed
        into networks of throbbing life-lines, streaming
        amniotic oases and a Chaplinesque affair
                        of the blood, where savage
                jabs and gestures joyously abandon
                                horizons:

But in a curated forecourt
there are two self-portraits enclosed
by sadness in shadows, cloistered
doubts brooding in spidery
saffron and cadmium yellow lines—a languorous
gangly untidiness worn by slippered feet.

Shout Out

to the revolutionary, twentieth century sculptors:
Margel Hinder, Inge King & Norma Redpath

I am home, out of work/out of friends, besieged
        though dreaming
a day out, thumbing a lift
through NGV guides whilst listening to tv news; and in the US
it's mid-terms, and the teflon comb-over shouts
      at guardians now stuck
          his other-fish-to-fry:

I hate
      this imperfect
vessel of a damaged god, lifting
          indecency high
as Christians (some my own family) rally
      against *Safe*
            Schools:

Seeking haven, I surrender to the gravity
of a *Symphony of Sorrowful Songs*, a holy
bowed minimalism moving stepwise
        downwards to folk
        drone and lament,
a soprano's soaring supplication
                breaching
    Gestapo cells, and I wonder
              how would Trump
              handle her...

It's almost
Remembrance Day, and in memorials, boys get all
the work, a stampede of lesser gods
        and adolescent fantasies where the slain
        are recruited, spread eagled
on their shields; and in gardens, potent voracious fauns
                are hard at it, abandoned to Dionysian urge:

        In former times the gang got bronze
to work on men: explorers, generals, gods...whist the odd
         hot Circe could be taken
to vows at the altar and liberated—
             a nude water nymph, waiting:

Wanting exception, it was time in 1972
        so, the RAAF commissioned Inge to rise
          through adversity to the stars
with three ground, stainless-steel monoliths piercing
        ANZAC Parade, machine polished
        milky way reflectors,
            but these open skies soon offended
uniformed men who came down hard
        medals flaring over chests:

        In this reserve
precious is male and bronze, but abstractionist
measurement in new material
irresistible: Margel, Inga and Norma's velvety smooth finish
of flat angled planes; their mobile cut
of fuse wire and soft solder; all those
truncated organic forms in ripe profusion of stone; Margel's tutelary deity
as mother and child carved
        from ironbark; Inge's stainless-steel rings of Saturn:

Now, full growth
is honoured by Norma in a heavily furrowed, (gender) neutral
bronzed dawn sentinel with 'trump' ballast
shed; now, with Margel and Inge, she expressively
textures beads of molten metal fashioned
by her welder's arc and leaving iron
exquisitely wrought like thistledown.

Song of Songs

for Jillian

I am no Bond, James Bond   with a little finger so clever
          others blush
I have pivoted to a slump   poor-John
                    a dull-witted suicide saved by light
love flooding in like enchantment
even if I still tote a trunk of nagging
          mixed reviews
          a happy-horseshit dalliance
          with the sober/meek
                    long black and lemon cake
          since martini whimsy
is in me a bumbling
                    dilettante's swing into the rough

And love shakes me like a
tear drop   a blossom falling
                              apart

          Can I open
to you, Jillian   my dove   will you linger
I am wilting in your hands
                    to your tongue
          can I stir   can I love enough to cherish you(r)
pulsating satisfier
                    to witness
          your banquet   afterwards holding
each other tight   I want
          back to your comely mouth
                              better
                              than any wine

Date Night

for Jillian

To her Facebook post I react
with 'love'. She has bestowed on me foundation
membership to the AFLW and tonight our Bulldogs romp
home in a Gandalf finalé of red, white and blue

On the big screen Lee Lin Chin cheekily
enthuses: 'women kicking balls, I'd love to
see that' as Ellie, Lauren and Brooke break through, clearing
the ruck after 'ball up' with a swooping step,
don't argue and bounce

This is game
on as the club, once a vice in overalls, sticks it up
him and hugs
a new guernsey

So, tonight we defiantly grandstand
our cheer, holding hands
as halves, whilst I take in the female
who has taught me   fair
rules of play

that kick, that photo

legs spread in pure

        unadulterated   airborne athleticism

                        eyes tracing the arc

to goal   such unladylike

        empowerment kicking balls and arse

and the unrelenting lament

        of trolls flown too close

to the light

of day

the most important, unimportant thing in the world

...each game day I promise no
booing, it amplifies
upset and (pantomime) paranoia
but when a run
of '50/50' umpiring calls blow
the other way, or that ex-captain
and his gang (quitters
for a cup) crunch
your smallest player, parasitical-wasps
hawk tails (and some), then you're a dog
in every grudge (they want to rub
you out) and halleluiah just becomes
a long-drawn groan
like boo...

Elgin's Marbles

(after Michael Scott's, Who Were the Greeks? SBS TV)

We hear him
quote J.S. Mill that Marathon is more important
in English history than Hastings, a conquest column
inscribed along a bronze helmet's rim
where victory odes gloat
in vinegar and blood broth
and those bitten by defeat
are forced to slink down alleys, shunned
like defect babies, where even the sacrifice
of dogs can't purify; and pankration wrestling is cryptic
prophecy where those disarmed
fight to the death; and drunken
centaurs and giants, in Persian dress, row
into the confusion of the straights
while above it all the Panathenaic Way
is a sacred olive branch gorged
on marble dust,
and gods are the spoils
of all our arts as a gold wreath rises
with the Parthenon in technicolor riot
over the humdrum; this is his television
radiant in the perfect proportions
of the male nude, but for women
a veil is worn,
while he casts the goddess
troublemaker, and his regret
is being blown off course
from the sanctuary of Apollo
at Delos where a monument to Dionysus
is armed as a good luck phallus.

We Are

...troweling through that God Almighty squabble
in a cross-sectioned trench that exposes
me, stretches of incorporeality
from now, back to conception and beyond
through all those Scottish/Jewish tradesmen and housewives (so righteous
despite the odd weed) with the occasional
rabbi and hell-fire-and-brimstone
Jew-for-Jesus thrown-in—what a jam
                              of blood

Finally reading Fagles's verse translation of
The Iliad (about time
the godly complaint) where a fairytale castle is studded
with coriander, cumin, rose petals, saffron and gold
and, while one young prince is obsessed with his
apples and all those glistening
love locks, another is the bulwark of shining nobility
but still, both are grassed
and placed at the head of a very long queue
where all are offered
the agonies of spilt brains and shaming
                              throbbing chants

Given by Gods
to black clouds of grief, shackled fast
to panic and taunted by years
of agony all for their terrible beauty—
                and Gods mutter amongst themselves

Flattened by these storm-cloud theologies
that shoulder crests, wave upon wave
surges of strife
tearing bronze; godly hordes of unceasing
vortex massing like flies over the holy aura of the hill, and from heaven
earth-shakers loosen disaster
where the sabotaged and judged
                    are weighed down...

The Dark is Rising

*a Peace Studies reading of Susan Cooper's fantasy sequence
reimagining Arthur & Merlin in modern times*

I am again hooked inside her prescience, escaping
airwaves bristling with a president's perilous night-time tweets:

How did this black hole wolf down
horizons, convert aspirants
into walls?

What is progress
    when we keep repaying
    hammer-blow malevolence, the festering
                resentments of a single bigot?
    how do we unriddle the stains left
        in the ground by an ancient hill fort, the long aching
lament for enclosure?

Susan Cooper (a child of war) went into the ground
       as air raid sirens wailed,
her mother reading aloud through the nights—
candle flame guttering
        at the impacts:

    So, Cornwall remains her windswept, craggy
seat of Arthur, a venerated realm
    of ancestors cleared of oak and hazel
            woodland, as those roused to chivalry
call upon the Blessed Virgin in a rush
        dealing death—souls breathed
                into winds:

But this menace need not be the only page turner
if we cast off 'Light' and 'Dark'
                        because, while prophecy
                poured forth fantastical wrath,
diggers can find no provocation
for a berserker boy-king
                in substantial and shrewd
                        well-to-do coexistence:

In these high stakes
        crusades between 'good' and 'evil'
                where a Round Table is ominous
                                and persistent in the reign
                of blood and dragons   we gorge
on the treacherous, convulsive lunge

                        toward smug isolation.

Judgment Day

for Susan Cooper & a reimagining of Ancient Britain

She knew Welsh and Cornish Chapel as prophetic and grim
standing stones, a hunched and fidgeting
earnestness without lightness:

But stains in the ground roused
in her the towering fancies of Logres as Arthur's Seat
where a citadel might just blaze
                         above chaos and plague:

For her, end times
are a Celtic seer, as a wild one is exiled in penitential urge
with dreams of mountains and valleys leveled, streams running
                         with blood:

As a trance medium (or latter-day novelist) she manages
monsters even as stones are hauled across sky-country
in a mid-winter journeying feast
                         of the dead:

And her Stonehenge is a portal
onto ancestors, with the living/recently dead assigned
henges of enormous oak timbers; rings of giants fixed
so that the hammerings and rapture of gods
                 can be left standing:

Here, Merlin is Great-Uncle Gummery with bristling
white eyebrows and fiercely curved beak-nose, no mere soothsayer
but a builder of henges, a craggy
and towering, hollow-eyed Indiana Jones in a high stakes,
                 coming-of-age battle:

Now the Dark's malevolence is at its Winter solstice
when the storm-cone is lashed
by Herne the antlered hunter
on Twelfth Night Eve, and the fierce-carved
                    quarry strides away:

And Greenwitch is women charming
a good harvest, where hazel and rowan prop the heavy sweetness
of hawthorn in the faint rim
          of perilous daybreak:

Here chapel might wish to censor
          magic, their eyes fixed on the beasts
of Armageddon, but beacon fires
          are lit and fluffy white clouds

                    are routed.

A Single One

(after Christopher Isherwood in LA, 1962)

I am still that small boy, taken in,
      life on the railway
                  tracks of the elect
and their anti-choice, revivalist crusades; I have shed
      religion but the stink
      is fear, a small boy immersed
in cinematic surround sound, excluded
        from the rapture and abandoned at the block
                      like a beast
      of Armageddon:

In their film for Jesus, the pulpit's megaphone
may as well be a submachine gun buffed
to shine since   there'll be no time
for sentiment after the bomb, and maintenance
      of a better type of shelter
           is as much a duty
    as daily devotions:

    In heaven, society is a hive
        and minorities   are feared.

An Earl Counts

(Written in the voice of Lord Bertrand Russell)

Dreaming comes from much worrying,
foolish talk from a multiplicity of words.
For every dream, a vanity to match;
too many words, a chasing of the wind.
Therefore, fear God. (Ecclesiastes 5:2-6)

Like the boy, Ares
I have contrived strife
100 books oscillating
                pendulum-like
between the Mad Hatter
and a scolded, avuncular Whig aristocrat striding
      dreamlike over his barren moors:

      The epitome
of privilege, I have given away
my freedom, so absorbed with the passion
to correct herd instincts; and from their confinement
of conscientious objectors I ascended
like a child, tirelessly noisy, playful
              and grubby:

      My faith
cast in absolute logic and the random
scatter of reality has become a trenchant shilling-shocker,
and a Bloomsbury fracas to escape loneliness
(to my shame)
has exalted me above the wake
        left by my paths to intimacy:

        At the midmost point
of a century's utilitarian balance sheet, finally they stood
cheering my Nobel, despite white anting
moralists whose graven images
            of fear were spun as wisdom:

And my tawdry 'chair
of indecency' became infuriatingly
a doctrine of free-thinking, the final
synthesis of mathematical logic where the ironically cocksure
could advance Socratic dialogues
            piece by piece and provisionally.

The Climate at Wentworth Falls

after AR Ammons, & Charles Darwin in the Blue Mountains
for my kids & their families (who are also drawn to mountains)

I followed Darwin's Walk again this evening
      to the falls,
from the ridgetop's open forest,
          contouring
    round the furrowed boughs of black ash
  and the smooth pale stands
of peppermint and blue gum flaking
      over banksia, mountain devil and waratah:

      Zigzagging
     down to the over-
        cliff track where
    clumps of button grass
     and holly-like grevillea bloom
  among the sedges of hanging swamps,
soils like peat collecting
along shales and sandstones,
    the sponged seepage zones
      of a fernery's rare collection:

    And along to the lookout at the falls:

Here a bushfire haze still burnt
over the escarpment's western rim whilst drizzle
      swirled around the fire tower
   like a halo, an answered prayer pledging
to starve the conflagration of oxygen and heat:

But this change was forecast
to a rattled line of spoiling towns
threaded along the railway and Great Western Highway,
        the length of a labyrinth's clear-felled, central ridge:

And while, after the rain, the blackened trees might once again
shoot green, the grasstrees fired
into flower, here
the industrial offering of sclerophyll is a knotty and wiry
garden of corpses
and pockets of virgin forest touched
                        for the very last time.

Animal Liberation

I: Hounded

for Charlie Brown, my first rescue greyhound

I was the dregs hitting the floor but still
I could cup the palm
of my hand over your cranium, fingers scratching
that spot
behind your ears, courting for you
a ceasefire in this alien
space of comfort & love & treats

What mass grave
of neglect might have been yours
after a life unsuccessfully racing, when camera/lights/action
are whittled down to a cage in a concrete pen

You came to me biting
yourself, your face a host of tics & yawns, too scared
for outside—the trace
of misuse

And yet, in saving
you, our self-harming is more or less
unneeded
& in my townhouse turned kennel
we are becoming
safe

II: Sir Jay Jay Raids Rich

for Billy Blue, my second rescue greyhound

raced   for the punters
a homebred genuine stayer   hooked
                out wide for speed star spoils

& his trainers manage the racing
                agenda   after deep pockets fracture
    his accessory carpal bone

to get him back
on track   surgeons   amputate
        front right toes

Sir Jay Jay is out there
        a distance superstar   rent asunder
                from the field

but a hundred grand in prize money is stillborn
        when it comes to post-racing care so a hobbled
    champ   is up for grabs

as Billy Blue he is my knight
                in shining brindle
    velcro-hound   snoot to snoot   limping from

treat to soft toy squeak
        these new-fangled lures lugged to a den
    now his snooza snuggler

                long-haul dog-love   redeeming   Charlie & me

Symphony in Tardis Blue

(On July 21, 1969, Apollo 11 landed in the Sea of Tranquility
as Neil Armstrong stepped out onto the lunar surface
he took with him a recording of Dvorak's 'New World Symphony')

Before the mercilessly spiteful steamship of state
packed with an army of cloned, robot WASPs and hurtling
into a black hole, Xian Zhang (regenerated as The Doctor)
exchanged her sonic screwdriver (which was so
twentieth century) for a baton that charmed

Beginnings: the melancholy gesture of violas
a little agitated section from woodwinds and haunting
cellos before the startling riposte
of timpani signaled a restless
journey in time and space; at once

Removed by an octave, double basses bowed
with bass clarinets and cor anglaise to clear
centre stage for the graveness
of clapsticks and a didgeridoo's droning
stomped defiance; before the ominous

Interruption of trombone and horn
a marching pitiless fanfare in robotic shells
the recycled themes
of heartbreak bitterly lingering
through a manifesto's Four Movements

Dvorak had been warned
against Black Arm Band melody
there was, he had been told, tragic majesty in salt
pans and arid hearts, a bio-diverse paradox
of recycling in impoverishment and fire

But Dvorak had heard the first people: Harold's soulful
echoes of darker memories in the cane fields; and he had wept
at Ruby's gravelly goodness down city streets; thus, he was compelled
to dream a symphonic bulletin washed in that blind river
song, Gurrumul: such angelic clarity sent packing

So, Xian Zhang coaxed, dipped and soared
as from her baton came propulsive resistance
to a command culture's mass-cloned
pietism, and formidable purity was uncovered
with vast expressive charge

Dvorak scored history in melodies and while once
his scrawled moniker met with such thunderous
applause that he bowed in his box like a king
here the sham of pepper pots was a cramped
and sweaty, 'contamination' intolerance

Prosecuted in a Doctor's opening night
                              sleight of hand

Spring Symphony

for my daughter, Ceinwen, who took me to 'The Planets'
a train our preferred carriage
after Gustave Holst & the Hammersmith Socialist Choir

So now she takes me by the hand, leading me
    out the door to ramble
              into Sunshine:

Every garden bed blooms
oranges, mauves and pinks, while lawns
are studded with soursob yellows and the dandelions' airy
white globes:

Nature strips are an upright haunt
of flowering gums, paperbarks and callistemons; while casuarinas
are encased in deeply furrowed, dark, hard bark
with canopies of wire-like
foliage and inflorescences grouped in whorls
            forming short cylindrical spikes:

Such a harvest
of seed and honey eaters, and above
it all—a Tullamarine flight path and daylight moon:

Exiting the station early we cross the Yarra for more gardens
a picturesque land where purple pea has been cast
            a life line in the ark, and we are free:

She takes me to bronzed pathfinders
    where a male nude is a hammer thrower in action
    while a female nude is *still* a reclining water nymph, waiting:

But her impatience subsides
　　　into childhood at *Genie*, a kitten fantasy
　　　where delight has wings, and other children now
climb and play:

At Hamer Hall we ride escalators
down to glittering
sunken walls where anticipation is a crystal
　　　　　　　　　　　pulse and flicker:

Seated in this concert hall, my back is that little bit straighter
　　　in my vintage Footscray guernsey
　　　　　　　　because to soar with Holst
was once a hymn for the Hammersmith Socialist Choir
where 'This Hath I Done for My True Love'; whilst sacraments
were the kneeling Red Vicar as Christ Militant
　　　　　　　swinging in the bell tower—remember
the victims of a bleak midwinter:

Holst ached for redemption, calling workers
　　　to arms, orchestrating brass bands and socialism
with his trombone from a bicycle saddle:

In this concert, a movement of bodies
　　　is a symphonic haunting　　of us all;
though Mars is a storm
where chromatic major triads sprawl
across staccato, and the slow heave of bassoon and horn
is a defeat in growing menace; but Venus is peaceful, resigned
　　　　　　　nostalgia, sighing
with relief as Neptune's wordless and off-stage female
　　　chorus recedes to eternal silence:

And in memory
of Jupiter's jollity
I am in tears, bustling
currents of shifting
stress, adjusting a hitched-up
spirit once again held

in a daughter's hands.

Set Shots

Ekphrasis:

Cactus is a collection of, by and large, Melbourne-based confessional & ekphrastic poetry. And while I explore what it is to live with poor mental health, I owe a debt to acknowledge the relief that I find in family, sport, the arts & Sunshine. This collection contains responses to the Fine Arts, the performing arts, literature, museum exhibitions, TV documentary, film, sport-as-performance-art & AFL collector cards. My poetics has always had as its cornerstone an experience of place. My place is now Melbourne's suburb of Sunshine, & such cultural institutions as the National Gallery of Victoria (NGV), Melbourne Museum, Hamer Hall, the Melbourne Cricket Ground (MCG), Docklands Stadium & Whitten Oval—I am so lucky to now call these places 'home'.

As I write these 'set shots' I am very sensitive of my old bendy legs. You can visualize any number of after-the-siren match winning goals, but for me, the soundtrack has to be right—the acoustic (or dirt music) of contemporary classical, jazz & bluegrass styles.

Acknowledgement of Country: 'Sky-Country':

When the Kororoit Creek Sculpture Walk was planned, I was lucky enough to be commissioned by Donata Carrazza to write a poem to accompany the site. 'Sky-Country' is the result. The sculpture walk is called *Spirits of Time and Place* & is the work of Melbourne sculptor, Geoffrey Ricardo.

'The Sunshine Line':

In 2018 Melbourne Museum hosted the remarkable exhibition, *We Call Them Vikings*. This exhibition invited us to move beyond popular (& Wagnerian) stereotypes, and to understand the peoples, once known collectively as Vikings, as migrants and small farmers. It also sought to educate that 'Viking' was not something you were, but something you did. To be i-viking was 'to be in viking', in piracy.

Excursions to this exhibition became a regular treat as I revisited such documentaries as Neil Oliver's, *Vikings* & Time Team's, *The Giant's Grave: Fetlar, Shetland Islands*. To be led to a reading of this rich history as being part of the long story of multiculturalism was delightful; & forever changed my journeys through Melbourne's West. My travels inevitably paused at Peter Corlett's sculpture of 'Mr Football' (a tribute to EJ (Ted) Whitten: a bronze sculpture with painted uniform and team scarf, located outside the main entrance to the offices and ground of the Western Bulldogs Football Club). This poem also makes reference to one 'Bulldog Charlie': this, of course, is Charles Sutton. Sutton was captain/coach of the Doggies in 1954 when we won our only twentieth century VFL/AFL Premiership Cup. In 2016 we repeated the feat, winning our second title—our club was founded in 1883.

My soundtrack while writing this poem was Henryk Gorecki's, *Symphony No. 3: Symphony of Sorrowful Songs*. This Polish symphony, in three elegiac movements, is a haunting reflection on motherhood and separation through war. Harmonic minimalism is not to everyone's liking, however, and one critic at the premier apparently loudly exclaimed 'merde!' after listening to twenty-one repetitions of an A-major chord. While another critic summarized the symphony as 'dragging on through three old folk melodies for an endless fifty-five minutes'. Several poems in this collection were written to this soundtrack (the recording I have is by the London Sinfonietta conducted by David Zinman with Dawn Upshaw as soprano).

'The Passion of Cards':

My struggles for good mental health are not easy (&, yes, terribly & indulgently melodramatic). I am my own worst enemy. Family is precious. The Doggies are also a clarion call not to do myself so much mischief. I have been lucky to encounter a psychologist (Martin Axelsson) who intuitively knew this. He got me substituting grog for footy cards—so wondrously canny. On my way to Melbourne's Card Zone (& Steve Wang), I often pause at Flinders Street Station to bask in my newfound safety outside a pub, & wonder at Mirka Mora's Flinders Street Station Mural.

'Bacchus In Ruins':

Bombing during the London Blitz exposed a Roman temple that was originally dedicated to the Persian god, Mithras, but was rededicated sometime in the third or fourth century to the crowd favourite, Bacchus. The starting point for this poem was my discovery of the BBC documentary by Bettany Hughes, *Bacchus Uncovered: Ancient God of Ecstasy*, & Anne Carson's verse translation of the Greek Tragedy by Euripides, *The Bacchae*. Bacchus was a boundary crosser, & was often pictured as a transgender idol—our inclusive/provocateur hero. I was also very lucky, during the planning of this poem, to discover the Yorkshire folk duo, Belinda O'Hooley & Heidi Tidow. They wrote the theme music to the gender fluid/lesbian drama blockbuster, *Gentleman Jack* (set in nineteenth century Yorkshire). O'Hooley & Tidow also wrote the hit single, 'Summat's Brewin' (oh Good Ale)' that celebrates the joy of grog. This song became my soundtrack while writing this poem. My mum, without ever being doctrinaire, is tea-total (having come from a long line of 'problem drinkers & gamblers') so I didn't have my first drink until around the age of 21 or 22, and from the time of that baptism I unfortunately never looked back.

'Hymns of Thanksgiving at the Existentialist Café':

This poem owes a debt to that grand old source of religious anguish as philosophy, Soren Kierkegaard, & to Sarah Bakewell's brilliant introduction to existentialist philosophy *At the Existentialist Café: Freedom, Being and Apricot Cocktails*. This poem is also, however, my hymn of thanksgiving to the music of Philip Glass, especially pausing over his film score for *The Hours,* & works for piano. In praising Glass, it riffs & paraphrases from a number of bluegrass favourites: Massive Attack 'Teardrop'; Mandolin Orange 'Wildfire' & 'Time We Made Time'; Sara Watkins (with Chris Thile & Sean Watkins: Nickle Creek) 'Destination'; Buffalo Springfield 'For What It's Worth'; Gillian Welsh 'Revelator'; & Sarah Jarosz/Jedd Hughes 'House of Mercy'. My soundtrack while writing is fundamental to my process.

'The Moment of Death':

This is brutal in its honesty, it hurt to write & is painful to read, so I might eschew the family history now, & focus rather on the aesthetic context & motivation for writing this poem. I love minimalism; whether this is a painter such as John Coburn, Mark Rothko or Sean Scully; or a composer like Philip Glass, Henryk Gorecki or Vladimir Martynov. And I am much attached to Kronos Quartet, especially their recordings of Henryk Gorecki's 'String Quartet No. 3' & Vladimir Martynov's 'The Beatitudes', 'Schubert-Quintet' & 'Der Abschied'. I loved minimalism before being ambushed by grief, but maybe this has given the obsession more urgency.

'Unforgivable':

How can depression be judged as sin? But, in conservative theology, despair is the 'unforgivable sin'. With pastoral care like this...

This poem is 'me' in a sentence. Proverbs 28: 14 says: 'Happy the man who is never without fear, he who hardens his heart will fall into distress'. My heart must have become 'hard' indeed. And, yes, I can hear (quite rightly) my psychologist & my partner's counsel: I am more than my depression, but sometimes I am ashamed to admit, this is very difficult to remember. I am 55, have no income, & almost no prospects. I am a teacher, much respected by nearly every student & parent I have worked with, but am now unable to teach until a psychiatrist clears me as safe (to myself). And I am barred from operating heavy machinery like buses, trains, trams & trucks (despite holding a heavy vehicle license for over 20 years with no demerit points). I am a danger to myself, never to others, but I am on the scrapheap. Depression is as humiliating as it is debilitating. My soundtrack while writing this poem was Nickel Creek's (Chris Thile, Sara Watkins & Sean Watkins) 'Reasons Why', & Sarah Jarosz/Jedd Hughes's 'House of Mercy'. I was feeling quite fragile while writing this poem, & these contemporary bluegrass classics reminded me that the flipside of despair might be hope.

'kith 'n' kin':

How do you confess that the only reason you have not passed away by suicide is that you dread too much the hurt left behind? My mum's dad (a hero of the Kokoda Track) died in an accident at work when my mum was seven. After this tragedy my mum, along with her four siblings, were removed from their mum and placed in a children's home at Burnside, in Sydney's inner-west. My mum is one of the kindest & most generous people you could ever meet, but she began her life in shit. She married dad and began her own family, like we were life buoys, and had six happy kids. But two of these died in accidents as young adults (exactly ten weeks apart) and so the cycle continued. I cannot explain depression (nor the guilt load left by suicide attempts). It is something that toxically spits & burps away like some old fart/geyser. I survive for my family, I wish I wanted to live for me.

'Gongoozler's Lament':

At the beginning of the British industrial revolution, but before the age of the steam engine, the most efficient way of connecting the industrial mid-lands with ports was by human (navvy) dug canal and horse drawn narrowboat. During the eighteenth and nineteenth centuries more than 2000 miles of canals were cut throughout the UK, but in the modern era of rail & road transport, this investment boom in canal construction ended, & canal maintenance went into serious decline. In the late-twentieth century there was a renewed interest in canals due to an explosion in leisure & residential craft. Today the canals have entered a new boom era. I first encountered UK canals via such books as LTC Rolt's *Narrow Boat* (1944) and the BBC documentaries: *Canals: The Making of a Nation; Great Canal Journeys* (by Timothy West & Prunella Scales); & *Britain's Best Canals* (by John Sergeant). I then spent many hours enjoying YouTube channels that celebrated a contemporary life spent permanently living on and travelling along the UK's canal system. I have become an armchair gongoozler (someone who loves being near water & watching boats but doesn't actively partake of the experience themselves). One of my new dreams, if I can overcome my fear of flying, is to spend a year or two with my partner in the UK, living on our own narrowboat whilst cruising the cut.

'What I Would Have Missed':

In late 2014, after my first suicide attempt, my perfect partner offered me the perfect bribe: get help & we'll upgrade our Doggies memberships to gold (this, of course, secures you first offer on finals tickets). So, in 2015 I located a GP who specialized in men's mental health, got 'off' the grog, & joined Sons of the West (a physical & mental health program offered by the Western Bulldogs). Our club also offers Daughters of the

West & Bulldogs Pride (& my Rainbow family is committed to all three initiatives). In 2016 our men's team broke a 62-year drought by winning the club's second VFL/AFL premiership cup; while in 2018, our women won their first AFLW premiership cup. I couldn't believe my luck, to have grand final tickets to the two most perfect games ever played—but, of course, I couldn't help also tearing up at the thought of what might have been (if my plans had not been interrupted). Hawktail is a young American ensemble phenomenon that fuses bluegrass & contemporary classical styles. This band, which is a distinctly American take on the traditional European String Quartet, consists of Brittany Haas on fiddle, Paul Kowert on double bass, Dominick Leslie on mandolin & Jordan Tice on acoustic guitar; it formed after my 2014 breakdown, so has become another obsession, reminding me to stay committed to my recovery, & to be a little kinder to myself.

'one-legged dog':

I love Mickey Rourke in *Sin City,* but his starring performance in Darren Aronofsky's *The Wrestler* is heartbreakingly wrought. This film responds to dangerous hurt/risk taking & self-harming in males as symptoms of socialisation in a culture of toxic masculinity. And Bruce Springsteen's closing song is perfect. I am not a big fan of pop or rock as a genre (so high on performance and low on content) but this pared back, acoustic performance brings me undone. The image of a 'one-legged dog' comes from the Springsteen song. When Springsteen wrote this song for the movie, he copped some abuse for the apparent incongruity of this metaphor, people unable to appreciate its bitter/sly quality. It, therefore, had to be my title. I am much indebted to Aronofsky & Springsteen for their reimagining of the disintegration of masculinity.

'Dark Matter':

I love dirt (or acoustic) music, especially bluegrass & classical. Many of my musical discoveries are made whilst listening to Washington's National Public Radio (NPR), which broadcast a series of Tiny Desk Concerts. Gillian Welch & David Rawlings, well known for their dark ballads, are just two of the summits in the American acoustic music community.

'A Valetudinarian's 'Crisis' in a Time of COVID19':

Punch Brothers is an American progressive bluegrass band made up of Chris Eldridge (on acoustic guitar), Paul Kowert (on double bass), Noam Pikelney (on banjo), Chris Thile (on mandolin) & Gabe Witcher (on fiddle). Music is a vital part of my life, and along with my family, has got me through many tough spots. Unfortunately, I am not always grateful of their help, which I sometimes confuse with meddling interference—depression is a stink.

'Unhinged':

Mummies Alive: Buried in a Bog is a documentary that aired in Australia on SBS TV. It examines the issue of failed kingship/king sacrifice in Iron Age Ireland. It led me to reflect on issues around masculinity, and the pathology of self-harming, since there was the suggestion that these kings, despite being drugged & bound, went willingly like Christ to their fate. Self-harming & suicidal thoughts are something that I have struggled with for a long time. Doctors & psychologists view self-harming as symptoms of mental illness, & while I'm sure they are right, their explanations seem inadequate. For me, self-harming has often been the only healthy way of surviving periods of mental health crisis; it leaves me relieved & calm. And popular culture, especially professional male sport, often sells messages that esteem sacrifice & dangerous hurt as a necessary part of success and bravery. A film that powerfully inhabits this space is Darren Aronofsky's *The Wrestler*, starring Mickey Rourke. Attempting to unpack these paradoxes remains urgent in my mental health care. I cannot pretend to have any insights into what this experience is like when you add homophobia, racism, sexism & transphobia, so I have confined my attention to myself.

'On Crying Wolf':

You don't commit suicide (as in to commit a crime) rather you pass away from it (as in from a car wreck). But, unlike a car crash, the causes of depression are very hard to forensically unpick. The arts, & especially writers like Virginia Woolf & Stevie Smith (who suffered so terribly from depression themselves) are haunting consolation. In this space, David Hare

& Stephen Daldry's film adaptation of Michael Cunningham's novel, *The Hours*, leaves me very fragile (it really should come with a warning)—& Philip Glass' score is like the aftermath of self-harm/shame relieved in a partner's arms.

'Flash Art':

Rosalie Gascoigne has been a passion of mine for a long time so when I met 'Flash Art' (1987, tar on reflective synthetic polymer film on wood) in the NGV, the meeting had to become a poem. And Gascoigne's title is so delightfully resonant with irony.

'Splintered Assemblage':

Rosalie Gascoigne: I wish I were one of her assemblages. I love all of her work, but my favourite has always been 'Monaro' (1989, synthetic polymer paint on sawn and split soft-drink wooden crates on plywood, Art Gallery of Western Australia). For a long time, I knew this astonishing assemblage only in reproduction, but in early 2019 I had the chance to travel to Perth, & meet this work in person. Whilst there I also introduced myself to 'Hung Fire' (1995, retroflective road sign on wood, Art Gallery of Western Australia). George Mackay Brown is a wonderful Orkney poet (1921-1996) who, like me, self-medicated for much of his adult life with grog's sly mouthful. Ursula K Le Guin (1929-2018) is a bestselling American poetry, fantasy & science fiction writer. She is perhaps best remembered for her *Wizard of Earthsea* books. This poem also owes a debt to: Christopher Allen, *Art in Australia: From Colonization to Postmodernism* (Thames & Hudson, 1997); & Vici MacDonald, *Rosalie Gascoigne* (Regaro, 1998).

'Call Me Legion':

In early 2019 I was lucky enough to visit the Art Gallery of Western Australia where I met, for the first time, Stanley Spencer's series of paintings, 'Christ in the Wilderness'. This encounter led me back to the Art Gallery of New South Wales and to Spencer's monumental, 'Christ in Cookham (Christ calling his disciples)'. I have loved the work of this twentieth century English painter for a long time, and often wonder what he would make of the church today. Not a conventional Christian,

Spencer probably would have described himself as a fellow traveller with the Christian socialists. As I planned this poem, I also reread Shusako Endo's novel, *Wonderful Fool* (1959): this is a brilliant reimagining of 'Christ' as a French traveller (& wise fool) in post-war Japan. I also spent a lot of time with Richard Heathcote & Anna Jug (ed.s), *Stanley Spencer: A Twentieth-Century British Master* (2016); & Kenneth Pople's classic: *Stanley Spencer: A Biography* (1991).

'From Hans to Nora, with Love':

The NGV exhibition, *Brave New World: Australia in the 1930s*, made graphic the inter-war battle lines where cultural rejuvenation was often sought in muscular nationalism & the eugenics of race reproduction. Many conservative commentators, however, took the view that these ideals were being shattered by the rise of the 1930s 'modern woman', a more serious & emancipated version of the 'giddy 1920s flapper'. The art from this period, therefore, often depicted women as either Venus/Madonna (that sacred vessel of maternity) with curly headed child, or Diana/Hippolyta of the hunt and battle where the prototype female body was lean, muscled & formidable. There are also many portraits from this period showing the rise of a new class of sophisticated, urban woman. Max Dupain summarized the thoughts of many at the time concerning the rise of this 'modern woman' when he wrote that it would result in a 'great shattering of modern values'. It was Dupain's judgement that: 'in her shred of a dress & little helmet of a hat, her cropped hair, & stark bearing, the modern woman is a sort of soldier...It is not her fault, it is her doom'. As a father/daughter artistic duo that spanned the generations involved in this battle for the 'ideal woman', the Heysens are a fascinating case study, inviting renewed attention & reappraisal.

'I Am the Vine!':

This sequence responds to the potent presence of vitalism in early twentieth century Sydney. If the sources are Friedrich Nietzsche & Henri Bergson then the (distinctly odd) conduit is Norman Lindsay. The vision is often a copy of Classical Revivalist, Art Deco, Symbolist & Art Nouveau tendencies. It impacted on all the arts, but was especially important to painting, sculpture, photography & poetry. It is, in part, a reaction against Great War horrors, and is celebratory of life-affirming/energized bodies, impulse & sensation, but is also a great hater (& is typically anti-feminist, anti-Semitic, anti-wowser, anti-religion, anti-modernist, anti-nationalist...). It advocated strongly for concrete imagery and was opposed to obscurity & abstraction.

In his book, *T.S. Eliot, anti-Semitism and Literary Form*, Anthony Julius argues: 'Anti-Semites are not all the same. Some break Jewish bones, others wound Jewish sensibilities. Eliot falls into the second category. He was civil to Jews he knew, offensive to those who merely knew him through his work. He wounded his Jewish readers, if not the Jews of his acquaintance, to whom apparently, he was not disagreeable'. Norman Lindsay was an anti-Semite like TS Eliot. My Pa was quite distraught when I showed him some of Mr Lindsay's writings on Jewish people, as he had always known such a polite and gregarious 'gentleman'. The cowardice of racism?

I have felt compelled to engage with this art that is still so prominently featured in most Australian galleries & libraries. It is so much bigger than just the dynamo of Norman Lindsay. And while some reputations have lessened over the years (ironically, that of the Lindsay clan, for instance) others have continued to prosper. Some of the inspirations for this sequence are: Deborah Edwards, *Stampede of the Lower Gods: Classical Mythology in Australian Art* & Denise Mimmocchi, *Australian Symbolism: The Art of Dreams*.

**'Prologue: When Jews for Jesus Call on the Oracle of Springwood'
& I: 'Springwood Olympus'**
Norman Lindsay (1879-1969): From a twenty-first century viewpoint, understanding the magnetism of Norman Lindsay, is almost unfathomable.

Max Dupain, for example, described him as 'that grand old man...of radical Hellenism...who inspired us all in his revolt against the god-awful bore of the mob'. While Ken Slessor wrote: 'It is a paradox, indeed, but none the less a fact that Norman Lindsay has exercised more influence & produced more effect on numbers of this country's poets [and artists] than by any other single individual... My own debt to his powerhouse of stimulation & suggestion is obvious'. It must be noted, however, that Slessor was also critical of Lindsay's 'thundering pronouncements'. Douglas Stewart also cautioned against hagiography, pointing out Lindsay's 'sometimes domineering ideas', & argued that Lindsay should be viewed as a 'fountain' of 'stimulus' rather than 'influence'; but he also observed that Lindsay was 'the outstanding figure, both for the brilliance of his artistry & the prodigality of his output... he was a genius'.

Lindsay's home is located in the Blue Mountains town of Springwood and is now run by the National Trust as The Norman Lindsay Gallery & Museum. The specific source of these two poems is Douglas Stewart's *Norman Lindsay: A Personal Memoir*.

II: 'Homer's Sorceress'

Bertram MacKennal (1863-1931): an Australian sculptor who lived much of his adult life in England. MacKennal was part of Auguste Rodin's movement of New Sculpture where the formality of Neo-Classicism was rejected in preference of new principles: idealized naturalism, modeling, touch & dynamic vividness. This poem responds to three of his sculptures: *Circe* (1893), *Daphne* (1897) & *Diana Wounded* (1905). *Circe* has long been a gallery draw card at both the AGNSW & NGV. The figure of Circe was the favoured 'femme fatale' of nineteenth century Symbolist art. MacKennal captures her dramatically in the act of witchcraft, transforming Odysseus' crewmen into swine. MacKennal was an international triumph, & not a follower of Lindsay, but he certainly influenced many Australian artists who did travel on the Nietzschean/Lindsayan path. My source for this poem is Deborah Edwards' monumental study, *Bertram MacKennal*.

III: 'Goulburn Odysseus'

Sydney Long (1871-1955): a painter of classical themes & landscapes in the Art Nouveau & Symbolist styles. Long is another LGBTQI artist sabotaged by homophobic & unsafe socialization.

IV: 'A Satyr's Thumbs-Down to a Laughless God'

Frank (Guy) Lynch (1895-1967): a Sydney sculptor, originally from New Zealand, whose sculpture, *The Satyr*, located in Sydney's Botanical Gardens has long been a crowd favourite. Guy was the brother of Joe Lynch, whose death on Sydney Harbour inspired Ken Slessor's poem, 'Five Bells'. My sources for this poem are the writings by Peter Kirkpatrick on the Lynch brothers in *The Larrikin Streak* & *Australian Dictionary of Biography*.

V: 'Sunbaker'

Max Dupain (1911-1992): a photographer influenced by Lindsay's ideas, especially on vitalism & eugenics. One of his most famous photographs is *Sunbaker* (1937). The specific sources for this poem are the collection of photographs in the book, *Max Dupain's Australia,* & the PhD thesis of Isobel Leila Crombie, *Body Culture: Max Dupain & the Social Recreation of the Body* (University of Melbourne, accessed online). Crombie shows that while Dupain is often celebrated as a modernist, he should actually be seen as a classical-modernist; his attitudes towards modernism being quite ambivalent. He often wrote, for example, of the 'degenerative' tendencies in modernism and disliked the 'hybridity' & 'fake sophistication' he thought characteristic of urban living.

VI: 'The Boy, Ares'

Jack Lindsay (1900-1990): was the eldest son of Norman Lindsay and Katie Parkinson. After Norman left Katie (& their three young sons), Jack became estranged from his father until his early twenties when they 'reconciled'. Jack then employed his prodigious talents to become Norman's chief acolyte & propagandist for his myriad of Nietzschean/Classical Revivalist/Vitalist doctrines. In 1926, Jack realized that he needed an 'utter rupture of the god-father fantasy', so left Australia for England, & never returned. In 1936 he became a communist & spent the remainder of his life advocating for an 'open' existentialist-Marxism. In over 100 books, Jack never deviated from his idiosyncratic, unabashed idealism. Perhaps his philosophy can be summarized in the concluding sentence of his biography of fellow utopian communist dreamer, William Morris: 'If the earth is not to be a radioactive waste, it will surely become...Morris' garden and forest'. My sources for this poem are: Jack's three-volume autobiography, *Life Rarely Tells*; Bernard Smith (ed) *Culture & History: Essays Presented to Jack Lindsay*; & Paul Gillen (ed) *Jack Lindsay: Faithful to the Earth*.

'Epilogue: Aphrodite's Renaissance'

Judith Wright (1915-2000): as I wandered around art galleries and libraries, with this sequence on my mind, one 'key' to understanding became my picture of Judith Wright as a student & young woman at Sydney University in the 1930s. In tracing Wright, I discovered how this decade saw the rise of a new Modern Woman as a more serious & emancipated version of the 'giddy 1920s flapper'. The NGV exhibition, *Brave New World: Australia in the 1930s*, celebrated this phenomenon while also documenting some of the reactions that rallied against it. Georgina Arnott in her biography, *The Unknown Judith Wright*, examines how as a young student at Sydney University, Wright became one example of this provocateur, a 'Modern Woman'. Arnott shows how Wright's exploration of the 'taboo subject of female desire', her preoccupation with the innate emotional & sexual connection between a woman's body & the natural landscape, began in her student days. And, in *Preoccupations in Australian Poetry*, Judith Wright critiques the presence of Lindsayan/ Nietzschean vitalism in early twentieth century Sydney poetry. My reference to the 'voyage out' is, of course, a tribute to the 'Modern Woman' through Virginia Woolf.

'Where the Bee Sucks':

John Olsen is another artist that I have loved for a long time, and this affair is also a little rocky. I was excited when news of a major NGV retrospective to be called *The You Beaut Country* was announced, but unfortunately, buying a season pass also led me back to Olsen's memoir, *Drawn from Life*. The sexist & homophobic values that Olsen displays in this book are dreadful. I am the father of LGBTQIA+ children, & while I am drawn like that tattered old moth to Olsen's art, I feel betrayed by the glare of Olsen the memoir.

When travelling to the NGV or Melbourne Museum, I begin by walking through my beloved Sunshine to the station, before catching the train to Flinders. I see beauty everywhere. In this poem I pause at John Kelly's stunning & comic 'Man Lifting Cow' (a bronze sculpture in Sunshine's CBD) & at the Russell Street Gates (these were once the main entrance to the Sunshine Harvester Works. The Scottish migrant and blacksmith, Charlie Pippett, constructed these gates in 1922. The gates are one of few surviving structures from the Sunshine Harvester Works factory).

'Shout Out':

In 2018-19 the NGV featured a small collection of work by sculptors, who from the 1950's, had challenged Australia's predominantly figurative sculptural tradition by creating abstract work. Margel Hinder, Inga King & Norma Redpath demanded a poem. Since the cost of bronze was usually prohibitive to these female sculptors, most of their work exists only as a maquette, or in less costly materials like stainless steel, stone or wood. This poem also owes a debt to: Ian Cornford, *The Sculpture of Margel Hinder* (Phillip Matthews Book Publishers, Sydney, 2013); Jane Eckett & David Hurlston, *Inge King: Constellation* (National Gallery of Victoria, Melbourne, 2014); Sasha Grishin, *The Art of Inga King: Sculptor* (Macmillan Art Publishing, Melbourne, 2014); & Mark Holsworth, *Sculptures of Melbourne* (Melbourne Books, Melbourne, 2015).

'Song of Songs':

When I am low, I have a canon of favourite films & albums to which I return time after time. Niall Johnson's, *Keeping Mum*, starring Maggie Smith, Kristin Scott Thomas & Rowan Atkinson, is one of these. It is often described as a 'black comedy', but is also a profound reflection on reconciliation, & is a joyful celebration of the Hebrew Bible's *Song of Songs*, sexual relations & family. It dances on a pinhead of sentimentality, without ever becoming banal, & is rich in a wicked, tongue-in-cheek humour. When planning this poem, I luckily discovered Sarah Jarosz & Chris Thile's cover of the hit song, 'Tear Drop' (by the UK Bristol Collective, Massive Attack), that featured on Thile's bluegrass program, *Live From Here*. This brilliant bluegrass/fusion cover, together with the more saccharine pop of 'Did You Ever Wonder Why?' (the film's closing song) by Dickon Hinchliffe (featuring Rowan Atkinson reading extracts from *Song of Songs*), became my welcome soundtrack while writing this poem. In both the film & closing song, Atkinson perfectly encapsulates the kind of tenderness & vulnerability that I am so drawn to when in need of mending.

'Date Night':

In 2016 my partner bought me foundation membership to the Western Bulldogs AFLW side. We competed in the first season of the AFLW in 2017 &, in 2018 (in pissing rain) won the second ever grand final: 4.3.27 defeating the Brisbane Lions 3.3.21 at Ikon Park in Melbourne. This was one of the finest days of my life.

'that kick, that photo':

In 2019, Michael Wilson took a photograph of AFLW star, Tayla Harris, powerfully kicking for goal from the fifty-metre arc. The image shows Harris in full flight, her right leg extended skyward, muscles flexed, eyes tracing the arc of the footy to goal. This iconic image of the AFLW has since been immortalized in bronze by sculptor, Terrance Plowright. The image, aptly titled 'more than a kick', went viral around the world as soon as it was released online, inspiring pride & excitement. The award-winning photograph also, however, provoked a flood of horrendous online trolling & sexually abusive misogyny. Reflecting on the photograph & sculpture, Tayla Harris has said: 'it's a pretty surreal feeling, it's more than me just kicking a footy, it's a message, a turning point'. I was raised in a church culture that esteemed sexism as received wisdom and as a consequence, to this day, I struggle with disrespectful & non-inclusive instincts. Sport & art can be a powerful clarion call for change.

'the most important, unimportant thing in the world':

I no longer drive (one strategy for helping manage my mental health challenges) so I am often on the train between Sunshine & the city. While on this commute, I have on several occasions, witnessed a fellow passenger's suffering while in a psychotic rant. I have also heard these desperately sad episodes from fellow patients while in a psychiatric ward. It is very confronting how often these monologues become misogynistic, homophobic & racist. Booing at the footy, inexcusably, can release similar passions. Fortunately, at Australian sporting stadiums, there are now healthy education programs to encourage the reporting of such anti-social behavior.

'Elgin's Marbles':
Michael Scott's *Who Were the Greeks?* is a documentary that aired in Australia on SBS TV. Scott is an affable, self-assured, English classicist turned celebrity.

'We Are':
In early 2019 I was gifted a copy of Robert Fagles' verse translation of Homer's *Iliad*. Fagles' writing is a magnificent page turner, so richly evocative & dramatically colloquial. There are few who could match Fagles in perfectly balancing the academic demands of an acclaimed translation with the potential of a best-selling potboiler. Discovering Fagles led me back to the BBC documentaries by Bettany Hughes (*The Ancient Worlds: Helen of Troy*) & Michael Wood (*In Search of the Trojan War*). I also reread the work of the great American socialist classicist, MI Finley, especially pausing over *The World of Odysseus*. I am not an atheist (I am far too indecisive to ever commit to such common sense, & I fear the distress this position would cause some of my family) but, like Iris Murdoch, I would describe myself as a Christian Agnostic. My soundtrack while writing this poem was Deborah Conway/Willy Zygier's brilliant & savagely satirical single, 'G-D' from their album, *Stories of Ghosts*. This song demolishes the idea of a loving God by highlighting the 'reality' of the 'All-Powerful Yahweh' (the 'I Am' of the Hebrew Bible) whose credence is judgement & pure vengeance: 'in the day of reckoning there is little kindness'. This poem inhabits these spaces.

'The Dark is Rising':
I am a big reader of fantasy novels. I've never taken to science fiction and post-apocalyptic genres (as a child I believed in the emotionally abusive

rubbish of a Christian Armageddon) but I reread all my fantasy gods every few years. Of course, from a Peace Studies perspective, the instinct to respond to the world in binary opposites in a way so characteristic of much fantasy literature (dark/light, good/bad, saved/unsaved) is non-inclusive & pernicious. This poem responds to these tensions.

My starting point for this poem is Susan Cooper's *The Dark is Rising* (a sequence of five novels that reimagine Arthurian & Celtic mythology into mid-twentieth century Cornwall & Wales) but I also owe a debt to such BBC documentaries as: Alice Roberts, *King Arthur's Britain: The Truth Unearthed*; Neil Oliver, *A History of Ancient Britain*; & such Time Team episodes as: *Journey to Stonehenge: Durrington Walls; Bodmin Moor, Cornwall: In the Shadow of the Tor*; & *From Constantinople to Cornwall*.

'Judgment Day':

This poem is another tribute to Susan Cooper's fantasy sequence of five novels, *The Dark is Rising*, but I also owe a debt to Alice Roberts' BBC documentary, *King Arthur's Britain: The Truth Unearthed* & Time Team's *Journey to Stonehenge: Durrington Walls*. My soundtrack while writing this poem was Sean Watkins' brilliant satire of American Protestant end-times theology, '21st of May'. Watkins perform his contemporary bluegrass classic with Chris Thile & Sara Watkins in their band, Nickel Creek.

'A Single One':

As a child I remember my family's church hosting, perhaps annually, a series of 'left behind' genre films. These films were part of a wider preoccupation with 'Christian Zionism'. And what this 'family entertainment' lacked in wonders & joy it abundantly made up for with an abusive & didactic obsession in spreading fear. Every film ended the same way: those excluded from the rapture (every woman, man & child) would have to choose between the 'mark of the beast' (a tattooed '666') & the chopping block. The stench of these childhood memories mean that I still do not like dystopia as a genre. I do, however, love Christopher Isherwood's novel, *A Single Man*, & for me, Tom Ford's film adaptation is as equally powerful. Ford heightens the dystopic nightmare of Isherwood's reaction against homophobic bigotry. I am the proud father of LGBTQI children, & Isherwood/Ford shine an anxiously hopeful light.

'An Earl Counts':

As a teenager & young adult I was a cliché of sincerity & fervent curiosity. I listened to Christian music from the American Bible Belt by stars with such names as: Evie, Family, Nancy Honeytree, Living Sound, Randy Matthews, Larry Norman & Randy Stonehill. I taught Sunday School & ran youth groups. I even handed out 'how to vote' cards for Fred Nile's Festival of Bigotry & Gloom. I come from a long line of tradespeople, preachers & rabbis, being the first person in a large extended family to win a place at university. When I anxiously began my study of history & philosophy, one family elder gave me a copy of Bertrand Russell's, *Why I Am Not A Christian*. My inoculation, however, against the evils of secular humanism has not gone according to plan. This poem is an expression of gratitude to Russell, and owes a debt to Russell's popular writings on ethics & moral philosophy, & to Caroline Moorehead's monumental biography, *Bertrand Russell: A Life*. My title is, at least in part, ironic given my history of boorish rants against royalty, aristocracy & the putrid privilege of their conservatism; Russell is my exception that proves the rule.

'The Climate at Wentworth Falls':

This poem was written after one of many jaunts along the Charles Darwin Walk at Wentworth Falls, located in the Blue Mountains of NSW. It is my hymn of thanksgiving both to Darwin & the great American poet-scientist, AR Ammons. Ammons is a big influence on my writing, and I have also long loved the journal that Darwin kept while on his voyage around the world on the Beagle. In it he records the details of his visit to Sydney in 1836, and how he travelled on horseback across the Blue Mountains, stopping at Wentworth Falls. I included a much earlier version of this poem in my first collection, *Sweetened in Coals*.

'Symphony in Tardis Blue':

Classical music is so often disparaged as belonging to conservative & privileged elites, so it is nice to be reminded of how progressive some composers like Antonin Dvorak actually were. While naming his ninth symphony the *New World Symphony* is an unfortunate legacy of colonialism, it should be remembered how much respect Dvorak showed

North American First Nations & Afro-Americans in researching & composing his *Symphony No. 9*. My poem is an attempt to have some fun & imagine what might have been if Dvorak had explored the Australian colonies (& Australia now) on his way to New York in the 1890's. If Dvorak had been commissioned to compose a symphony for Australia, I don't think our army of cloned little-Johns would have been too pleased with the results. I wrote this poem after attending the Melbourne Symphony Orchestra's performance of *Symphony No. 9: New World Symphony* at Hamer Hall & conducted by the dynamic Xian Zhang, September 24, 2018.

This poem has Dvorak meet three outstanding First Australian artists: Harold Blair (1924-1976) was a tenor & activist, born in Cherbourg, who at the age of two was separated from his mother & raised in a Salvation Army Home; Ruby Hunter (1955-2010) was a singer/song writer who collaborated with Archie Roach (her partner), Paul Grabowsky & the Australian Art Orchestra to create the musical, 'Ruby's Story': a celebration of Hunter's resilience and joy in life after surviving the anguish of the Stolen Generations; while Geoffrey Gurrumul Yunupingu (1971-2017) was a much loved and celebrated Yolngu singer/song writer from North East Arnhemland.

And which episode of *Dr Who* is my favorite? Well, that's easy: None. I am not a big *Dr Who* fan (though I am the odd one out in a family of Whovians) but I love *An Adventure in Space & Time* (BBC, 2013): a biographical television film celebrating the creation of the *Dr Who* phenomenon, and ABC's *Whovians* hosted by Rove McManus.

'Spring Symphony':

On September 1, 2018, I was given one of the best musical experiences of my life. My daughter, Ceinwen, fulfilled one of my wildest dreams by taking me to a performance by the Melbourne Symphony Orchestra of Gustave Holst's *The Planets* at Hamer Hall. Ceinwen is an artist & art therapist, so is always treating me with such special experiences; she also took me to Punch Brothers when they visited Melbourne. I am one much loved & very lucky man.

I have long adored Holst (such majestic music composed by a utopian communist dreamer), listening to many recordings of his works—especially

The Planets—and have sought out introductions to the man & his music: Imogen Holst, *The Music of Gustave Holst* (Oxford University Press, 1968); *Classical Destinations II* (Decca Music Group, 2009); & *Holst: In the Bleak Winter* (Isolde Films for BBC, 2011). Holst composed his symphony, *The Cotswolds*, in memory of the English Pre-Raphaelite communist, William Morris. And he served as conductor of the Hammersmith Socialist Choir, where he would meet his future wife (Emily Isobel Harrison), which was sponsored by Morris' Kelmscott House Socialist Club in Hammersmith. Holst loved Morris' communist utopian novel, *News From Nowhere* (1890), and would continue to search out the spiritual guidance of the Red Vicar of Thaxted (Rev Conrad Noel), who was vicar of Thaxted from 1910, where he was a prominent Christian Socialist.

Acknowledgements

I am enriched by the love of a large family, & am bound to them all, but I especially honour my parents, Ray & Joan, my partner, Jillian, & my four children: Rhiannon (& Jason Bardsley), Aidan (Jessica Esveld & my first grandchild), Ceinwen, Kian (& Brooke Collins)—the love with whom I fly.

As always, my first confidante & editor while writing *Cactus*, was Jillian Hall. I could do nothing without her generosity & expertise. Jillian has a first class honours degree in Early English Literature & Language from the University of Sydney & thus has an eye for detail & syntax that so enriches the writing produced by my ADHD brain—I am very lucky to have my life partnership with her. We begin most Saturday/Sunday mornings slowly with Bluegrass/YouTube narrowboating while enjoying together David Astle crosswords over coffee. We also often use this time to collaboratively play around with my poem titles, & many of my titles are the product of this creative partnership. I have also received much encouragement and insightful feedback from Kian & Rhiannon Hall. Kian is a genius of experimental & speculative poetic & prose fictions/dramas, & Rhiannon is a much-loved English teacher in Sydney's South-West where her obsessions include doctoral studies on complication & voice in YA verse-novels while also running creative writing clubs for her students.

Since early 2018 I have met monthly with Anne Carson, Tom Clark, Anne Elvey, Paul Fleckney & Rose Lucas to read & discuss each other's work. And they have so improved my poetics of ekphrasis & place (both geographical & interior/psychological). I am very lucky to have met such insightful care & generosity.

In early 2019 I was invited to attend a Southern Highlands poetry group to workshop this collection's opening poem, 'The Sunshine Line'. I am greatly indebted to: Rhiannon Hall, Peter Lach-Newinsky, Anna Kerdijk Nicholson & Greg Tome.

My poetry has always been autobiographical & place-based, but since moving to Melbourne's suburb of Sunshine, my poetics has been greatly enriched by regular conversations with Kris Hemensley: AR Ammons & William Stafford; William Carlos Williams, Lorine Niedecker &

Objectivism more generally; the San Francisco Renaissance/Beats; Black Mountain; The New York School; & the early 'Confessionals': John Berryman, Elizabeth Bishop, Denise Levertov, Robert Lowell, Sylvia Plath, Anne Sexton & WD Snodgrass. The recent developments in my poetics owe much to Kris' remarkable generosity & acumen. Regular conversation with Kris & Loretta, at Collected Works, is a treasured bonus of life in Melbourne.

The first people to read *Cactus* from 'top-to-toe' were Donata Carrazzo & Martin Dolan, & I am greatly indebted to their generous & insightful reading of my work. Donata is the Chair of the Mildura Writers' Festival Committee, while Martin is a poet & editor with Recent Work Press.

In late 2018 I was honoured with a featured reading at La Mama Poetica, in Melbourne, & I am very grateful to Amanda Anastasi for giving me the opportunity to first read publicly a selection of poems from this book.

In 2020 I published two essays in *The Blue Nib* which included a generous selection of poems from this collection. These essays reflected on what it is like to live with poor mental health, some of the links between thoughts of suicide & creativity, & the debt I owe to my partner, Jillian Hall, & my rescue greyhounds, Charlie Brown & Billy Blue. I am thankful to Clare Morris, Denise O'Hagan & Dave Kavanagh for their encouragement. The essays can be found at: https://thebluenib.com/hounded/ & https://thebluenib.com/the-allure-by-phillip-hall/

Poems from *Cactus* have been previously published in: *The Blue Nib, Burrow, Cordite Poetry Review, Overland, Plumwood Mountain: an Australian Journal of Ecopoetry & Ecopoetics* & *RECOIL.*

I am so relieved & joyful to be included on the Recent Work Press list (& so, so appreciative): Lisa Brockwell, Martin Dolan, Penelope Layland & Shane Strange—wow, thank you!

The first person I ever met, for whom the arts were something that you could centre a life around, was Graham Abbott. Graham is a violist & conductor (& respected Handel enthusiast). He was also for a time a much-loved presenter on ABC Classic FM where he pioneered the program, *Keys to Music.* Graham was my teacher in secondary school & something about him soaked into my spirit. I have been enriched & better ever since.

About the author

Between 1987 & 2014, Phillip worked as a teacher of sport & camps throughout regional NSW, Far North Queensland & the Northern Territory. He designed sport & Outdoor/Environmental Education programs designed to teach emotional resiliency, cooperative group learning, safe decision-making & respect for Country. In late 2014 some unresolved mental health issues reached a crisis, & he suffered a breakdown which resulted in a period of hospitalisation & the end of his career. In late 2015 he retreated to Melbourne's Sunshine where he could concentrate on his recovery while 'working' as a writer. Phillip has completed (via external/part-time studies) a Doctor of Creative Arts at Wollongong University where he researched Australian poetry, contemporary place theory, ecocriticism & postcolonialism. For many years Phillip has published his poetry, reviews & essays in such spaces as: *Antipodes, Best Australian Poetry, The Blue Nib, Burrow, Cordite Poetry Review, Meanjin, Meniscus, Plumwood Mountain, Overland, Southerly, Verity La* & *Westerly.* His books include: *Sweetened in Coals* (Ginninderra), *Borroloola Class* (IPSI), *Fume* (UWAP), & (as editor) *Diwurruwurru: Poetry from the Gulf of Carpentaria* (Blank Rune Press). Phillip is a passionate member of the Western Bulldogs Football Club (& a foundation member of Bulldogs Pride).

Printed in Australia
AUHW022203260622
365514AU00008B/28